DUST AND
Diamond

Poems of Earth and Beyond

DUST AND
Diamond

DONN TAYLOR
Author of *The Lazarus File*

A Division of WINEPRESS PUBLISHING

Pleasant Word (a division of WinePress Publishing, PO Box 428, Enumclaw, WA 98022) functions only as book publisher. As such, the ultimate design, content, editorial accuracy, and views expressed or implied in this work are those of the author.

Scripture references marked NASB are taken from the New American Standard Bible, © 1960, 1963, 1968, 1971, 1972, 1973, 1975, 1977 by The Lockman Foundation. Used by permission.

Scripture references marked KJV are taken from the King James Version of the Bible.

ISBN 13: 978-1-4141-1141-4
ISBN 10: 1-4141-1141-X
Library of Congress Catalog Card Number: 2007941472

... for dust thou art, and unto dust shalt thou return.
—Genesis 3:19

In a flash, at a trumpet crash,
I am all at once what Christ is, since he was what I am, and
This Jack, joke, poor potsherd, patch, matchwood, immortal diamond,
Is immortal diamond.
—Gerard Manley Hopkins

To the memory of my father,
Dr. Walter F. Taylor, Sr.

He was a man, take him for all in all.
I shall not look upon his like again.
                    —*Shakespeare:* Hamlet *1.2.187-88*

Contents

Preface xiii
Acknowledgments xv
Notation xvii

TIMES, PLACES, PERSONS
Panhandle Dust Storm 1
The Rhine At St. Goar 3
Epigram: 1869 4
Pioneer 5
Isolt 6
Ear 7

MEDITATIONS
Beyond 11
Horizon 12
Reptiles 13
Thoughts On A Bridge 14
Beyond Physics 15
Power Outage 16
I Do Not Know... 17
A Birthday Acrostic 18
Married Love 19

BIBLICALS
The Raven's Complaint 25
Barak 26
Vin Ordinaire 27
Villanelle: The Death Of Hezekiah 29
Soliloquy Of A Youth Without Blemish 30

Rejection And Reward 31
Emmaus 32

PICTORIALS
Picasso: *Harlequin And Companion* 37
Tableau 38

OF WARS
Terminal Conditions 43
Patrol 45
Truce 46
MacDonald Carey's Eyes 47
Cosmos In Wartime 49
Blessings Of Peace 50
Seoul Olympiad, 1988 51
Wallflowers 52

RESPONSES
On Hearing W. D. Snodgrass Read His Poem
The Midnight Carnival 57
No Exit, Or 59
And This Is To Reply: 60
Epigram On Hebrews 13:2 (KJV) 61
The Dogs In Tamina 62

REGRETS
Training Ground 67
The Unephiphany 68
The Lost Ones 69

SATIRES AND PARODIES
Locusts 73
A Carol For Our Time 74
Fashion Models 76
Revised Standard 77

Stopping By Words In Escrow For Thieving 78
Precessional 79

LAST THINGS
 "A Fair Field. . . ." 85
 Bloom Of Almond 87
 Walk Into Daylight 88

Preface

These poems are written by a Christian living in a world that is fallen, yet holding in memory fragmented images of its unfallen state. It is a world in which we never get anything completely right and often get it completely wrong.

So this is not a book of pleasant devotional poems, although some do fit that description. These poems are best described as poems of experience, sometimes hard experience, though never of disillusion. (After all, our Lord confronted us with many hard realities which we would prefer not to face.) Certain poems, with the poet as the speaking voice, are intensely personal. Others, some serious and some humorous, adopt the voices of wrongheaded speakers and pursue their wrongheadedness to its logical conclusion. (This is especially true of the satires, and I hope we will remember that God created both irony and humor.) A few poems deal with literary or biblical characters, and one or two contemplate myth and mythic reality. But in all the poems I attempt to address things that are objectively true and things that are consistent with basic Christian doctrine. (If I did not believe that doctrine true, I would not be a Christian.) Not all the poems are directly Christian, of course, but all reside within the boundaries of Christian experience.

How well I have succeeded in these intentions remains for others to decide. But despite this overly serious preface, I hope readers will relax and enjoy the reading, especially of the poems in which humor plays a part.

In preparing this book, I owe special thanks to my brother, Dr. Walter F. Taylor, Jr., for his counsel based on depth of literary understanding; to Jackie Pelham and Linda Kozar for many helpful suggestions; to Dr. Guida Jackson and the late Bill Lauffer for innumerable helps over a number of years; to Wanda Dionne and Woodlands Writers' Guild for critiques and encouragement; to Terry Burns, Chip MacGregor, and

Athena Dean for leading me to WinePress Publishing; and to the many writers' conference conferees who have encouraged me to publish a book of poems.

Most of all I thank Mildred, my beloved wife, for her wisdom, inspiration, and continuing encouragement through the years; and Karen, Warren, Katherine, and Walter, for accepting their father's successive eccentricities as soldier, professor, and poet.

Acknowledgments

My thanks to editors of the publications in which the following poems were previously published: "Beyond Physics" in *The B.A.W.L. Point Pen,* June 2001; "Cosmos in Wartime" in *The B.A.W.L. Point Pen,* Jan. 1999; "The Dogs in Tamina" in *Houston Poetry Fest 1996 Anthology;* "On Hearing W.D. Snodgrass..." in *Touchstone Literary Journal,* vol. 21, Winter 1996/97; "Horizon" in *Presbyterian Record,* Jan. 1996; "Locusts" in *Touchstone Literary Journal,* vol. 20, 1995; "MacDonald Carey's Eyes" in *Poets' Roundup* anthology, 1997 and *Touchstone Literary Journal,* vol. 21, Winter 1996/97; "Married Love" in *Discoveries,* vol. 17, no. 2, Spring 2000; "Notation" in *The Lamp-Post,* vol. 21, no. 4, Winter 1997-98; "Panhandle Dust Storm" (as a prose poem) in *Suddenly* II, 1999; "Pioneer" in *The B.A.W.L. Point Pen,* June 2001; *Houston Poetry Fest 2007 Anthology;* "The Raven's Complaint" in *Christianity and Literature,* vol. 46, no. 2, Winter 1997; "Reptiles" in Poets Northwest's anthology, *Inner Visions,* 1998, and *The B.A.W.L. Point Pen,* June 2001; "Seoul Olympiad, 1988" in *Touchstone Literary Journal,* vol. 20, 1995; "Stopping by Words in Escrow for Thieving" in *The B.A.W.L. Point Pen,* January 1999; *"Vin Ordinaire"* in *Poets' Roundup* anthology, 1996, and *The Lamp-Post,* vol. 21, no. 4, Winter 1997-98.

Notation

What is man, that thou art mindful of him?
—Psalm 8:4 (KJV)

I am a single note, sounding but once
And not sustained, a transient passing tone
Too briefly audible for resonance,
One moment's quick vibration, quickly flown—
Not a suspension, bold to stand alone,
Alien and strange to the prevailing chord,
Subsiding into consonance, yet known
Distinct in selfhood. I have not explored
Some fresh key's flavor, nor can I afford
The thrusting dominant's drive to rest again
Upon the keynote, certainty restored.
I'm one slight scratch from the Composer's pen,
    Yet by that scratch preserved forevermore,
    One part of His divine eternal score.

Times, Places, Persons

Panhandle Dust Storm

Barn-battering blast of wind and dirt, this three-day storm
Brings terror to tin-roofed sheds, scours paint from walls,
Makes kites of aluminum siding and leaves them bent,
Bow-tied on telephone poles. It stings our skin
With pellets flung in our faces, buries our eyes,
Turns trees into train whistles mourning their loneliness
In a visible universe shrunken to fifty feet.

Our ears grow exhausted with sound, with skirling and crackle,
Scratch and spatter of gravel against our house—
A snapped antenna wire's whiplash, flaying the roof—
The stutter of fluttering shingles about to take flight.

This swirling of gray-brown dust has stolen the sky.
The stars are all fiction now, the planets extinguished,
Sun and moon dull silvery disks too feeble to glow.
The law of gravity's gone—the earth's in rebellion,
Dissolving itself into space as an ocean of dust motes.

Sea-surging, this wind comes in waves, assaulting the house
With breakers that pound and recede, then hammer again—
This house now a ship lost at sea, and leaking all over
While dust-streams puddle in corners in every room.

No weapon at hand, no way to fight back at this wind—
We've nothing to do but wait it out inside.
How long? Who knows? Till God grows tired of it all,
This showing a bit of His strength—decides to rest—
Restore repose.

Then soon, in quiet dawn,
With winds quiescent on the settled earth,
We'll wake to stillness and a tranquil sky.

The Rhine At St. Goar

No mystery here. The geographic facts
Suffice: Profoundly beautiful,
Restless, the river slides through the deep gorge,
Turbulent at sharp bends and yet benign
In blue reflection from the summer sky.
A lone barge train engraves its frothy *V*,
And white-walled buildings crowd the water's edge.
Above lie vineyards terraced on the bluffs,
Then sheer rock cliffs with ledges burgeoning green.
Beyond, a castle stands, and over all,
One jagged pinnacle of layered rock—
The factual scene today.
                              Yet once, they say,
A younger river in a world less bound
Brawled through this gorge. That ageless rock,
Promontoried above, aloof, alone,
Held watch in silence while the Lorelei,
In mists of shadowed evanescence combed,
Caressed her gold cascading veil of tresses,
Softly chanting strange harmonious tones
Of unknown timbre in an undiscovered key.

Epigram: 1869

Twin rails extend the reach of civil life
Westward until the continent is spanned:
Strange paradox, when slender strings of steel
Connect the oceans but divide the land.

Pioneer

No woods of Carolina ever bore
The weight of loneliness this prairie held.
She stood appalled: impossible to meld
This vastness to her finite flesh, ignore
Her sense of insignificance before
Such massive seas of grassy strangeness, quelled
In heart by brute immensity, repelled
That all she saw were sights she must abhor.
But then a lizard slithered in the dust
To gulp a bug and hide behind a stone.
A grackle pecked nearby, and both were sure
With instinct's certainty. She watched, alone,
And thought, "I guess I'm smart as them." She must,
She knew, if never thrive, at least endure.

Isolt

Alone in her dark tower at the head
Of those cold solitary stairs that led
Her from her love, no sooner found than lost
Without fulfilment or reprieve that night
The cold wind blew on Cornwall, and the sea
Beat out its lonely might against the stones
Of the bare cliff that stands forlorn, foreboding
There above—In her dark tower, alone,
She stands among the shadows, in despair
Darker than they, to gaze with violet eyes
Across the cold, gray weary sea that moans
And tosses endlessly beneath her tower.
Silent, she lives again forbidden love
And wonders where across that restless sea
To what far shores her Tristram finds his way,
And what lips now supplant her burning kiss.

 Ear

For Whittaker Chambers

After the decades of despair,
the storms of futile striving,
one daily commonplace
blossomed into miracle.

In her high chair
his daughter was eating.
His idle gaze rested upon her ear:
living resilience of infant flesh,
delicate complexity of curvature, infinite
pattern of perfection
and untold labyrinths within....

The miracle of her ear
burst upon his hardened heart
and suddenly he knew
that there is God.

Meditations

Beyond

feeling's meadow of mayflies
daytime playful azalea
clover in clusters, scythe-shy,
nighttime flickering firefly
seasonal swift-change, breeze-blown
redleaf, shimmering snowfall
yes, beyond—

from steadfast, staunch-stoned crag-high
mountains, massive, majestic—
mind-force aligned in golden
noon-blaze even at midnight,
beckons and beacons in constant
abiding lightning-bright ideas.

Horizon

In two dimensions all agree:
This circle marks our boundary.
A third dimension coincides,
Yet simultaneously divides.

For some conceive the world a bowl
Centered on the acquisitive soul;
Whatever falls within the brim
Flows inward and accrues to them.

But others find the world a sphere,
Themselves at pole; and they, from there,
Flow outward toward the planet's girth
With gifts of self, enriching Earth.

Reptiles

This purple lizard-shadow in my eye,
      Where vision used to be
Till some intruder blocked an artery,
Implants a ragged scar to vilify
Each perfect pattern with its roughly fret
      Reptilian silhouette.

Thus, once, another alien came to bate
      Or mar our inner sight—
To blend, with all that's beautiful, a blight.
To canker every good we contemplate,
He left a loathsome gift, with hue of coal:
      His cobra in our soul.

Thoughts On A Bridge

There on the bridge in Minneapolis
In that enchanted summer of my youth,
I gazed as green transparent waters flowed
Between white limestone cliffs. An August sun
Played on the glistening waters, sending reflections
Shimmering, etching a light-dance onto the cliff face.
Beyond the cliff a university,
And church bells, somewhere, joined in verity
To unify the scene: truth, beauty, joy,
Distilled in one bright vision, forever mine.

Two wars, four decades later I return
To gaze on waters blackened by pollution—
Dull, opaque—a highway paved in ebony.
No reflection now, no flickering interplay,
Though limestone cliffs, besmirched, still hover above.
Church bells are mute; the university
Has traded truth for relative morass.
No light, then, for the grime-corrupted scene:
Drab world motionless, all things draped in pall.

Where are we now? Is this the sunken trough
Between enlightened waves of moral height?
Or is this sullen state our human norm:
Becalmed upon a tasteless, toxic sea?

Beyond Physics[1]

The brute beasts dead, decayed before …

This factual flat scratch—
horsehair, tight-racked, dragged
on catgut stretched,
tortured from post to peg—

in Heifetz' hand

springs into glimmering silver
sheen of sentience, sending
promise of tones transcendent
singing from soul to soul.

---

[1] As a child, I heard a literal-minded comedian describe violin playing as "dragging the outside of a horse over the inside of a cat." Years later, I heard the Jasha Heifetz recording of the Beethoven Violin Concerto. In this poem I use the sound and texture of words to suggest both the difference between the two and the meaning of that difference.

Power Outage

After the ravenous winds
And the roaring of angry waters,
This muted sequel:

The wires are fallen now, as if to hush
Our clamor of engines,
Insistent decibels of every day—
Gone the compressor's whine, the whirring of fans—
Our civilization regressed
To pre-Edisonian dark
And stillness we hardly remember.
As when, in a concert's momentary rest, we hear
Heartbeats above our own suspended breath,
So now we hear
Whisper of quivering leaves,
Insect's affricative, redbird's tingling fife—
Minutest world of elfin micro-sound.
Our spirit, too, awakens once again
To sounds inaudible except for souls
In deep reality
Revivified.

All praise to Him,
Master of storm and silence,
Who smote the lesser power out
To let the Greater in.

I Do Not Know...

I do not know why I love you;
let it be enough that I do.
I do not know why it happened,
nor do I know when,
for this came no stroke of sudden force
bending me as a willow in the wind.
It came rather as the dawn
creeps westward slowly, softly,
fearful to disturb the lightest sleeper.
And though gradually I grew aware
of this mysterious aura, strange and luminous,
I did not wake to its wonder until
with fully opened eyes I gazed upon

the sun

pure bright and beautiful before me,
lighting the darkness of my heart.

A Birthday Acrostic

March 2005

Incapable to speak my heart's desire,
Longing to tell you all my heart can feel,
Only to find that words cannot reveal,
Victorious, the deep love you inspire—
Earnestly I ask your pardon now,
Yielding to tasks I find impossible—
Over, above my talent's meager fill—
Unless you deem sufficient this one vow:
Most of all, I will seek your happiness
In everything I do while life shall last,
Leaving lesser ambitions in the past,
Determined I will never cherish less—
Rather to demonstrate, while I draw breath,
Expressive acts that show my constant state:
Devoted to your happiness till death.

Married Love

Outside the house a steely rain falls cold
On frigid myrtles. Rooted in shale and sand,
Few, sodden blossoms struggle, some survive,
In burgeoning bramble's fierce embrace.
On slate the pelting raindrops tick like clocks,
Dissolve in sand and dissipate in streams
To merge in many a torpid pool. Cold rain
Holds all dominion here, though there are times
When geysers flaunt and fade, or tremors tell
Of dull volcanic muttering under earth.
Rain-glazed, the windows of the house reflect
A glittering horizontal leaden light,
Mirror mirages, mystify, perplex
Perspectives so that all beyond the glass
Seems insubstantial shadow. Dwellers here
Ponder upon this prospect—but with minds
Unpenetrating, pensively bemused
In bent reflections, wander once again
Their land of rain and sand and shale and rain.

Inside the house, frescoed above the hearth
With cherubim to bless his sacrament,
Triumphant Hymanaeus[2] wields his torch
Radiant with warmth and light; within his kerchief

---

[2] The god of marriage in classical mythology, as described by Vincenzo Cartari in the mythological manual *Imagines Deorum* (Lyon, 1581). I have modified Hymanaeus' iconography to portray marriage as a blend of classical and Christian tradition. The mythical god Hymanaeus is not the human heretic and blasphemer named in 1 Tim. 1:20 and 2 Tim. 2:17.

Borders of blue surround a crimson field—
Crimson contained in blue. Behind him rest
Three children sheltered beneath green olive trees.
Facing the hearth, but well within its warmth,
A fountain's waters fed from a freshening spring
Scatter in patterning eddies, endlessly varied
Crystalline cascades, fusing at last to flow
Deep to a single cistern. Near the hearth
Hang tapestries of blue with gold enwoven
Spinning wheels and pomegranates rich with seeds.
In window boxes blossoms burgeon. Light
Through windows many-prismed by the rain—
Light from beyond the clouds, beyond the skies—
Transforms the rain, the house and all within,
Transfigures whitened walls to blossoming gems
In infinite combination, shimmering tones
Of sardius, sapphire, emerald, beryl, topaz,
Amethyst, amber and onyx—laved in light,
The house becomes a jewel. Pondering here
On mystery's meaning, questing couples claim,
Secure, their sacramental diamond,
Height of this life, earnest of that beyond.

Biblicals

The Raven's Complaint

(Genesis 8)

I'm grateful, yes—he was a nice old guy—
The food and roost were fine, without a doubt
The best I'd known. And then he sent me out—
An honor: first bird back into the sky—
A chance to show my stuff—you bet I'd try
My best—I *was* grateful to him. What lout
Would do less? I flew my tailfeathers out,
Thought nothing of it, flew two weeks, kept dry
Above the flood, alone. But where's the credit
Good works and self-reliance ought to bring?
The dove flopped twice, came slinking back and took
The old guy's charity and then forsook
Him, yet he's made symbol of everything
Graceful, I of gloom—I just don't get it.

Barak

(Judges 4)

After fine words of prophecy,
Gray doubt crept in to quarrel.
I won the victory in the field;
A woman wears my laurel.

Vin Ordinaire

(Canaan: In the time of the Judges)

These are no vintage years; today we taste
An ordinary wine that wets the lips
But leaves the palate thirsting. Vapid lives
We spend on shallow commonplace concerns
And spiritless endeavors, inching on
In ruts of dusty habit toward some end
That yet eludes our vision. Empty skies
Spread endlessly above; this promised land
Lies languorous and spare. He comes no more,
Whose vibrant spirit through our vintage once
Infused His joyous purpose. In ourselves
We cannot rise in crisis: here within,
My neighbor flaunts his Baal; from without,
Raiders on camels plunder. Yet through all,
Old habits reign: even now my neighbor's son
Beats out his father's wheat in usual ways,
At the wine press under an ordinary oak.

In vintage years, delicacy and power
Commingled tang of purpose, Exodus, conquest,
Zest of destination! Skies broad-blazoned
Constant epiphany in cloud and fire,
Emblems of grandeur shouting His presence: God,
Master of plagues and pestilence, parted seas,
Of melodies too, and manna's morning miracle—
Trumpets and crumbling walls, suns held at halt,
And Sinai's barren crag quickened by lightning—

Stones burst forth into flame, and shepherds' staffs
Made flints unfold into fountains. False priests burned;
Justice clear: punishment or forgiveness,
Nothing between—

                                   But now He comes no more;
No purpose calls; no destination beckons;
Bushes burn in the ordinary way,
And dawn brings only dew. Thin wine for all:
For me, devout; my neighbor with his Baal;
Even my neighbor's ordinary son, Gideon.

Villanelle: The Death Of Hezekiah

Behold, I will cause the shadow on the stairway...to go back ten steps.
— Isaiah 38:8 (NASB)

Manasseh...erected altars to the Baals and made Asherim....
— II Chronicles 33:1-3 (NASB)

The shadow moving backward on the stair
Becomes prophetic: shadows now combine
To consummate the curse of answered prayer.

Dying, I prayed for life—time to prepare
The kingdom—God answered with His sign:
The shadow moving backward on the stair.

Those fifteen years He gave me brought an heir—
Manasseh, named *Forgetting,* young, malign—
To consummate the curse of answered prayer.

He stands among the shadows, waiting there
My death, to bring his idols, redefine
The shadow moving backward on the stair.

His shadows bring forgetting—men foreswear
Their great divine inheritance, made blind,
To consummate the curse of answered prayer.

The kingdom thus moves backward to despair
With shadowed idols. Symbols now entwine:
The shadow moving backward on the stair
To consummate the curse of answered prayer.

Soliloquy Of A Youth Without Blemish

(Babylon, 605 B.C.)

Out of that flux and instability,
This life dependable. On foreign soil,
Freed from the worship of a god grown old—
So weak that servants of the stronger gods
Swarmed thick as locusts in Jerusalem,
Looting the sacred places, heathen hoards
Forcing our youthful exodus—thus freed
From vain traditions wan and impotent,
We, favored youth, pursue new destinies.
Yes, for a while we feared our conquerors,
Feared that our lives were forfeit, sacrifice
For foreign gods, but soon we learned we'd been
Imprisoned into prosperity,
Led captive into contentment, privileged
To learn the lore Chaldean wise men know
And dine on delicacies we never knew
In our outmoded law. Yet there are four
Among us who, ungrateful, yet hold fast
To the ancient diet. Well, so let them be.
We, more adaptable, quick to conform
To customs of our hosts—eating their food
And worshiping strange gods of greater strength—
Will move ahead to greatness with their king,
Our names archived along with royalty.
And while we rise, the rebel four will fade,
Forgotten like their ineffective god,
Their names dissolved into obscurity—
This stubborn Daniel and the other three.

Rejection And Reward

(Jerusalem: In the time of the Christ)

In bitterness at their hypocrisy
I turned away. Hearts lifeless as a shroud,
They stood in streets and shouted prayers aloud,
Self-serving boasts of their authority.
Better to have no faith, I thought, than be
Tangled in webs of rules that they'd endowed
With Decalogue-like weight. And so I vowed
To go my way without their deity.

But then I saw a miracle performed:
A prophet, dust and spittle in his hand,
Restored a blind man's sight. I felt my zeal
Return. They called him "Master" and they swarmed
About him. Now I kneel before this man
In whose hands even dirt and spit can heal.

Emmaus

(Luke 24)

They walked the bleak road wearily, bereft
    Of all they held most dear.
Without His presence, who could persevere?
He'd brought them hope; without Him they were left
To face the rabble's taunting and disdain,
    Their master slain.

But then a stranger joined them on their way,
    A learned rabbi skilled
In prophecies their Master had fulfilled;
And later, as he broke the bread that day,
They gazed upon the One that they adored,
    Their risen Lord.

Still later, in Jerusalem, He stood
    Among them all to show
His risen self reality, and though
He then ascended, "all things work to good":
The Comforter He gave them to indwell
    Still guards us well.

Pictorials

Picasso: Harlequin And Companion

The masters teach us how to see
    subtleties we never saw before....

Until Picasso painted, who'd have found
    such psychic peril in companionship?

But there in his poignant painting
    they huddle, pressed close together, almost
        Siamese twins,
and stare with pained and pensive gaze at

        nothing—

He with nervous hands pulling at his face,
    thin lips locked tight,
Squinting into the glare of what might have been—

She, more quietly, resigned,
    resting her chin on the back of her hand,
Dreaming of better times—

Bleak tableau, no movement made
    except in memory and regret—

Yes, the master makes us understand:

    intimacy is sometimes like this,
      bringing us physically close
        yet all the while
    this closeness drives our minds great miles apart.

Tableau

Her pose bespeaks the fullness of her life,
This slender lady sheathed in blue chiffon,
Languid upon her cabriole settee.
Her dark hair dishabilles on shoulders smooth,
Unburdened by the weight of needless care.
She smiles contentment at the things she loves:
The purebred Bernese couchant at her feet
Upon the polished floor; a harpsichord,
Antique, to know light touches from her fingers
Now and then. White bookshelves on the wall
Display her Hummels—boy with violin
And girl with cello—several scattered books,
And on the highest shelf, a metronome.

The artist posed her well. But afterward,
Reflecting, did she smile? Or did she hear
The silent ticking of the metronome?

Of Wars

Terminal Conditions

Behind his wheelchair in the quiet dayroom
    his oxygen bottle murmurs. His breath
      sighs heavily and long.

The steps of his chair support his leaden legs.
    He forces stiff-fingered hands together,
        wills them to lift a paper napkin to his nose,
      then lets them fall.

He fights internal battles now, drafted again
    into an army that never grants him leave
        —long, losing wars
    with emphysema and with Parkinson's.

In the hall outside, three mindless residents
    wheel slowly, aimlessly by in time-blind circles.

His mind is quick: he skewers points in time
    and serves them up well done, concisely tells
        of Patton, Overlord and Torch; golf scores;
          the nurses he prefers; his sons' careers;
            New Deal and CCC; his granddaughter's prom;
      the fall of autumn leaves outside his room.

He tires, can't force the napkin up again, grows quiet.
    The oxygen bottle gurgles behind his chair.

New visitors enter the dayroom. Arguing briefly,
    their backs toward us, they switch the TV on,
        tuning it quickly to find The Game of the Week.

And while the veteran of Kasserine Pass
    dies slowly in his wheelchair at their backs,

they watch, entranced, as quick young players,
    protected by pads and brightly-colored helmets,
        within the carefully-chalked boundaries of a field,
          with diligent officials enforcing the rules,

      attempt to prove their manhood in a game.

Patrol

No greater loneliness than this
   As last light fades
   Gray cold seeps in
To stiffen mittened fingers.

Across the valley darkness blurs
   Moonscape trenches
   Into silent ripples, purple sea
Soon smothered, black-hooded night.

Time for a hand-flick signal
   Rifle bolt snickers
   Round in chamber, safety on,
Cheek-chill, night wind rises.

Valley obscure, full dark,
   Inward sigh, whisper into the cold
    Two words often penultimate,

"Follow me."

 *Truce*

(July 27, 1953)

This sudden silence
deep as halls of hell
between screams.

Sunrise, surreal dreamscape.
Beyond the valley
anthill swarms of those we knew before
only as shadows.

We ourselves
stand where we dared not crawl
until this moment.

Tingling bloodrush,
miracle of living
fazed by fatigue,
stained by grief
for friends not here to see.

Pang of regret
for work unfinished

by command.

And softly, like portentous
dull volcanic tremors
at the earth's foundation,

distant thunder, north, beyond Chorwon...

MacDonald Carey's Eyes

What has been is remote and exceedingly
mysterious. Who can discover it?
                    —Eccles. 7:24 (NASB)

Is there a place where unrelated otherwhens
Combine in unity? And are there times
When trickster time itself may half reveal
Mosaics made of moments harmonized
In purposeful design? Or do we dream
Completion?
               Here tonight I watch a film
From fifty years ago, familiar tale
Of cowboys and the law. I drowse, secure,
Till suddenly the camera closes on
MacDonald Carey's eyes, and barriers
Of linear time's illusion fall away:
As through a window to another world
Long dead, I see Rod Polburn looking through.

Rod Polburn—cocky, competent, and brash—
Who taught me Tay Ninh province, road by road,
Forced landing possibilities, the best
Escape routes, and twelve landmarks to define
The border that we weren't supposed to cross.
One hour each night, with photographs, cassettes,
And earphones, he would turn his back—revoke
The jungle and the engines and the guns
To visit with his family. Later on,
In Heidelberg, I paused a while to mourn
His crash in Georgia.

47

But narcotic time
Sedates us with its linearity:
Snows fall. Streams flow. We leave our dead behind.
We raise our families, pursue careers,
And build as best we can. Then trickster time
Coils back four times upon itself and strikes:
From Hollywood's Old West, Rod Polburn's ghost
Stares out into my living room tonight
Through MacDonald Carey's eyes.
                                        Is there a place
Where no lost *when* is *other*? Or a time
When pilgrims can awaken into dream?

Cosmos In Wartime

There at the center of the universe,
An ocean and a continent away
From where I labor, calm at end of day
Descends, drawn down by likeness, to immerse
Her house in tender truths till she rehearse
For children deep assurances that say,
"This spirit-night, no strife nor storm shall sway
These quiet cradles, nor the world amerce
Souls of these innocents for ancient wrong
As price for human essence wrenched awry."
She speaks in trust that only grace allows,
Modestly unaware her softness, strong—
Stronger than stone or steel—holds up this house
In love, to let the house hold up the sky.

Blessings Of Peace

"The Democratic Party brought peace to Vietnam and Angola."
—*Walter Mondale, televised campaign speech, October 1976*

One caucus in the House, one Senate vote,
And nations fell. Now in some placid plot
Where life once flourished, bloating bodies rot,
Bones bleach in fields, and fetid corpses float
In rivers rancid with decay. Garrote
And gun rule all, and in each evil grot
Of blood-smeared chambers, Red Armbands find what
Wrings screamed confessions from each tortured throat.

But rest, lost millions, rest consoled to know,
Though hope may not survive nor slaughters cease,
In this just world no sacrifice is vain;
For now this pleasant Presbyterian,
Smiling self-righteously from the video,
Can make his pious boast, "We brought them peace."

Seoul Olympiad, 1988

For Fred Grant

We watched it on the video, Fred and I,
Two tame professors past our prime; we saw
The resurrected city, watched with awe
Its five bright bridges, high-rise towers that vie
Proudly with clouds—clear proofs that could deny
The place we'd known: one pontoon bridge of raw
Rough steel, flat ruins where maimed adults would claw
Through filth for food, and half-starved children try
To last just one day more. Such memories brought
Yet more: ice, night ambush, terror amid
Stark muzzle flashes, dead-weight fatigue—Engrossed,
I asked, "Would you do it again?" Fred thought
A moment, spoke: "You bet your life"—then paused,
Thought, smiled, and said, "That's really what we did."

Wallflowers

She warms the cushioned chair along the wall,
This dowager with hands that knit or twiddle
Aimlessly. Her sad and ardent eyes
Seek out, vicariously, the vibrant young
Twirling within the dance with quickened pulse,
Immersed in their vital here and now. Her heart
Quivers to music as it did before
In warm-breathed summer days' expectancy,
Feeling the slide of dance shoes on the floor,
Strange hand upon the back, awakening touch,
And racing blood at chance caress of cheek,
Tomorrow's promise glimmering beyond....

Thus I,

Warming the softness of my cushioned chair,
Seek out on video our vibrant young
In foreign lands—Iraq, Afghanistan—
Steadfast in peril, proud in sacrifice
And service. Idle now, vicariously
I watch, clutching the poignant memory
Of days of usefulness that come no more.

Responses

On Hearing W. D. Snodgrass Read His Poem
The Midnight Carnival [3]

You caged the sun and gave us
poet's inverse vision,
carnival knowledge of your darkened world
of angels and obscenities
conjoined,
where *logos,* on the tattooed man,
in learnéd allusion and winning wordplay
deconstructs
into unimpounded doggerel,
fragmented phrases revealing
an *avant* with nothing to *garde.*

A sunless solar system
knows neither soul nor system,
no center to hold in orbit
willful planets wanton to plan it otherwise,
and in absence of attraction even
thought itself lacks gravity.

---

[3] *The Midnight Carnival* is a collaboration between Snodgrass and the painter DeLoss McGraw. Snodgrass's reading was accompanied by color slides of McGraw's primitive paintings. The first slide showed the sun imprisoned in a circus-wagon cage, a metaphor for the midnight world. The poem consisted largely of wordplay and odd conjunctions of sacred and profane. This poem imitates the technique in an opposite cause.

The Big Top stretches tentatively
canvassing midair
while netless tightwire walkers
exhibit *angst* unneeded,
for art
netting no gain,
grasping without *gravitas*,
affords no further fall.

In your house of mirrors
the cosmos, seeking its image, saw
a random numbers table,
nothing new,
for long ago
Tom Wolfe found your carnival in Piggy Logan's circus,
whose audience was often swine-dled
but never mystified,
and Dante in his dark wood knew
each man's true place is measured
in distance from the sun,
that in bleak Beatitude,
unblesséd are they who encumber the sun,
the forever unenlightened.

No Exit, Or ...

Separated from my house by a row of headstones
I simply cannot see where there is to get to.
The moon is no door.
          —*Sylvia Plath, "Moon and Yew Tree"*

I did not find it so the other night
When I, like she, alone in deep despair
Wandered among the tombstones, desperate heir
To timeless evil—guilt—the world's dark blight.
So must we ever agonize, contrite,
Smothered by this vast wrong, a wrong we share
By being here. Above, the moon hung fair,
A door to purity, a lure to flight.
And so it proved: it opened easily
On well-oiled hinges, and I slithered through
To greet a world unfallen—fresh, too new
To know of sin. Yet only briefly free,
I breathed its rapidly polluting air—
A world no longer pure, for I was there.

And This Is To Reply:[4]

All right, you ate the plums. And I suppose
   You think I'll just forgive you once again
   After an angry morning. Heaven knows
   I've let you off the hook for many a sin
   Like this. You look so burdened with chagrin
   It seems a shame to scold, and my heart melts—
   At least it used to. Not this time, my friend.
   Don't be surprised when you start feeling sick.
Those luscious plums you ate were laced with arsenic.

---

[4] With apologies to William Carlos Williams, author of "This is just to say/I have eaten the plums…."

Epigram, On Hebrews 13:2 (KJV)

Historically, some few have had their share
Of entertaining angels unaware.
Myself, I'd take a more inclusive view
And entertain their outer garments, too.

The Dogs In Tamina[5]

The dogs in Tamina walk with their palms upturned,
Soliciting tips for services not rendered.
Tails limp and languid, wagged by the wind if at all,
They bask in a binary bliss of sleep and sloth.
Why should they serve? Why struggle or fend for food,
When waiting works just as well, and Samaritans come
Contributing edible alms, all service-free?
These dogs never bark; they're laggards of laissez-faire
And practicing pacifists, unlike their junkyard kin
Who'll fight at the drop of a fat, or leap at a lean.
And Tamina dogs don't hunt, though unfettered by fences—
They amble in opiate apathy, dogs on the dole,
Somnolent supplicants steeped in the welfare way.

Pedigreed Woodlands canines behind board fences
Bark with their noses in air, tails stiff behind,
In hairy hauteur and hubris. Suburban chic
And ostentation prevail as they tend their turf,
Boasting of bloodlines deftly developed, defined
With each trait traced to its place in the twelfth generation.

---

[5] Tamina (rhymes with *stamina*) is an undeveloped rural area north of Houston, Texas. Directly across I-45 lies The Woodlands (line 14), an upscale suburban development. Dogs in the two areas have distinctly different cultures.

Tamina dogs have never been taught about turf
Or bothered with bloodlines, but if the truth be told,
Their bloodlines blend with the best, though genetically jumbled,
Containing all traits of all dogs for centuries back—
Back to some *Urtext* of houndhood, hidden in tangles of time—
Perhaps in Eden some airedale Adam once sired their strain—
Perhaps in a special creation, the Lord Himself
Said, "Let there be mongrels!" and mongrels emerged by the millions,
Multiplying like maggots, to litter the landscape,
Flagrantly fruitful, till competition compelled
Dispersion—a doggy diaspora! Wand'ring the world,
Some travelled to Tamina, settled and slept—but slowed
By metabolisms too muddy for movement, stayed,
To live by the law one pristine poet penned:

> Hope springs eternal in the canine breast,
> For scraps and morsels mongrels can digest.

Regrets

Training Ground

Above the children's playground in the mall,
One plastic tree with overhanging leaves
Blinks with its cartoon-animated eyes
And tells again in deep, recorded voice
Stories of much that people used to prize
In ages past. Beneath it, children play,
Leaping among the mushroom-audience seats,
Shouting and braving the brook to celebrate
Their quick young physicality—
Ambience of inattention, serving well,
Protecting pleasure from demands of mind.

And so in middle school as teachers toil,
Speaking of sums and substances and such,
Or teaching values prized in ages past,
Children respond in patterns learned before
In other training grounds, building their dreams
On things more relevant—athletic shoes
Or spiked green hair, ring-pierced anatomy,
Or last night's video games and MTV—

Most useful habit, one that serves them well,
Preserving pleasure into future years,
Immune to screams from each new holocaust,
Unmoved by inner pang, should conscience call.

The Unephiphany

They saw no star and heard no angels sing:
For them no light or song, but only stale
Continuum. Without awakening,
They slept content that ancient night prevail.
Unheard, by them, the knocking at the door;
Unseen, the way, the truth, the life. For them
The dead world dragged dead weight to nothing more
Than what had always been, a cosmos dim
In shadowed second causes, naught beyond.
Their kinsmen live today, and still they see
No star and hear no song and feel no bond.
For them, perpetual unephiphany—
   For eyes and ears cannot perform their part
   Without the willing opening of the heart.

The Lost Ones

(Psalm 68:6)

Here in the oasis it's hard to visualize
That place the lost ones name Utopia,
Created by their choices day by day,
And by their definitions, to become
The optimum of human habitation.
Truth, they say, is not inherited,
A thing already there that needs discovering
Through diligent research and reasoning.
They say that truth is "socially constructed,"
Which means they make it up along the way.
Grant them heroic effort to construct
Reality as they think it ought to be.
Grieving, we watch them wander there outside.
How strange it seems to see them eat the sand
And call it nourishment, or drink their own
Ideas, defining them as water—strange to see
Their search through stones for spirituality.
We didn't make the oasis: we found it here,
Fully created, all its terms defined
Within the boundaries of the Decalogue—
We'd only to discover and enjoy.
We beckon, but they turn their eyes away,
Defining oases as a superstition,
Preferring barren paths of sand and stone,
Seeking through alchemy, defining dross as gold,
Circling forever in the deserts of the soul.

Satires and Parodies

Locusts

Properly
worshiping diversity
we welcomed locusts when
they came by twos and threes
for though they ate from our crops
our labors provided a plenteous harvest
and locusts appeared so quaintly decorative
standing on streetcorners, miming in mirrors,
and naming themselves the lilies of our fields.
Then
soon
taking to heart their praises of our tolerance
we were beginning to gaze in mirrors too
among our labors, but slowly learned
locusts multiply geometrically,
and when our crops are eaten
quaint locusts prove our
schools and homes
also become
edible.

A Carol For Our Time

(To be sung to the tune of "Hark, the Herald Angels Sing")

Hark! The merchant anglers sing,
"All cash registers must ring.
Fleece an earth by ads beguiled:
Merchants' checkbooks reconciled.
Frantic, make the children need
Satisfaction for their greed."
While the merchant hosts proclaim,
"Making profits is the game,"
Sharp commercial hustlers sing,
"All cash registers must ring."

Churches, join the rush for cash!
Stage proud programs full of dash—
All competing here below:
Who can give the greatest show?
Glitzy costumes cost a pile.
(Charities can wait a while.)
Fill the church with sounds of pride;
Let the Christ-child wait outside.
While the members have their fling,
Pray cash registers will ring.

Graceless grinches, seize the time:
Make your propaganda chime!
Earthly songs are good enough:
Censor supernatural stuff.
First amendment as decoy,

Rid the schools of Christmas joy
Till God's trumpets douse the lights—
Then complain about your rights.
Meanwhile, carp and loudly sing
To glorify your caviling.

Fashion Models

To prove grotesque grows never out of style
   Nor blatancy blasé,
They stalk across the fashion floor
   In bold asymmetry.

They never scissor, but widen stride,
As heels like hooves replace the tap.
In leaden promenade they step
And stop, pivot, pout, glower,
Wither the crowd with visage sour
In garish garments to signify
Alternative philosophy.

Animal fabrics (*faux,* of course)
   Perforce project a feral feel
When draped about anatomy
   In casual dishabille.

Reversible boleros hide
And then reveal the underside,
Décolletage pretends esprit
With navel maneuvers not at sea,
And chignons closet in hats cloche.
Models never give up the gauche,
Lamé excuse, while some cavort
In flattened soles for summer sport

With other nymphs of sullen face
   To serve in substance, style, and tone
   Designers who have never known
The taste of either gracefulness or grace.

Revised Standard

At Sunday celebration
light flows in
through stained-glass windows
where Jesus blesses
children gathered at his feet.
In the sanctuary below
(now called the meeting hall)
celebration reigns with joyful noise
of trap drums, guitars, oboes and other instruments

amplified

decibels into deliration
shaking the church's foundation.
Walls tremble
stained glass shatters
Jesus falls out of the picture, leaving
children to bless themselves
while joyful celebrants
mirroring each other pursue
their pleasure of the day
without missing a beat.

Stopping By Words In Escrow For Thieving[6]

Whose words these are I think I know.
But since he wrote them long ago,
He cannot stop my stooping here
To steal his words when mine won't flow.

Professor Jones may think it queer
To find archaic language here
With current slang contaminate
And thoughts that only half cohere.

He'll give his head a little shake,
Deplore, bemoan, and bellyache;
But at his back grade deadlines creep:
He'll pass me through, the lazy flake!

Philosophy is dark and deep;
Its solemn thought engenders sleep,
And there's this date I plan to keep:
I'll crib my credits on the cheap!

---

[6] With apologies to Robert Frost, author of "Stopping by Woods on a Snowy Evening."

# Precessional[7]

God of all notions oversold—
    Lord of our far-fetched party line—
Beneath whose spurious spin we hold
    Dominion over souls supine—
God of Precession, hedge our bet:
When *we've* been wrong—make *them* forget.

Our vaunted visions melt away—
    Dissolve in consequences dire—
Our social plans of yesterday
    Sank Sidon first, then flattened Tyre.
Divine Spinmeister, save us yet:
That *we* were wrong—make *them* forget.

From our judicial blunderbuss
    Convicted felons rule the street—
And public housing, thanks to us,
    Makes Hiroshima's ruins look neat—
Lest we get caught in our own net,
Lord God of Spin, make *them* forget.

We purged hard subjects from the schools—
    Self-satisfaction taught instead—
Producing unemployment pools
    Of graduates dumber than the dead.
Lord God of Boasts, flim-flam them yet—
Though *we* were wrong, make *them* forget.

---

[7] With apologies to Rudyard Kipling, author of "Recessional."

Of promises, we've launched a hoard,
	More than our actions can redeem—
Protect our reputations, Lord,
	But more than that, our self-esteem—
Don't let *us* languish in regret:
All damage done, let *us* forget!

When angry minds assess the blame
	For all the plagues our plans have loosed,
And we propose excuses lame,
	Don't let *our* chickens come home to roost!
Our just desserts, help us avoid:
Brand all our critics paranoid!

Last Things

"A Fair Field...."[8]

"I don't look that way often," says my neighbor,
"This field demands attention. At my feet
So many wonders glitter that my eyes
Draw down to earth—each blade of grass
An emblem, life triumphant, and this trumpet vine
Circles its bush and vaults into the treetops,
Binding in gleaming green of symbiosis,
Blazing in orange bloom. That single squirrel
Scampering, arcing, leaping across the lawn—
Instinctive ecstasy and pride of life—
Is miracle enough to ground my thoughts
In duty here. What tragedy to lose
Even one species! Thus my day is filled
With deep concern to keep right ratios
Of worms, wolves, and woolies. So that strange
Enigma yonder can't compete. That's why
I don't look that way often. When I do,
It seems a mirror where I see myself."

He finds this path I journey on too narrow,
Hedged on either side by poisoned thorns
Of "Thou shalt not." Yet from this place I see
His field entire, but in a different light
Revealing all its pleasures and much more
Beyond, above. And while these hedges guide,
My path lies clear before, inviting me
A few more reasoned steps before it turns

8 In the allegory of William Langland's *Piers Plowman,* "A faire felde ful of folke"
   represents the world.

In ways I can't yet see, or drops away
Through valleys of a depth I don't yet know—
Perhaps, at times, to unimagined heights.
It's mine to follow, confident, secure
In destination. Light is different here:
That's not a mirror but a window there,
To show vague shapes and tantalizing forms
Of glorious things beyond, assurances
That there, all turnings done, at journey's end
The mystic window will become a door.

Bloom Of Almond

Low, low, dark harbingers of that unknown;
Soft, spirits of the shadowed veil;
Gentle be my going forth,
In silence my cessation.

    For the almond tree has flourished
    The sound of a bird awakens,
    The sun, the light, the moon and stars are darkened,
    And the pitcher has been shattered at the well.

Through all my decades in this fallen world,
Through all the blood and terror of man's wars—
Wars between nations, greater wars within
(The ravages of seven deadly sins),
And these most savage wars within myself—
Haunted by helplessness for each new holocaust,
Through all my ten thousand transgressions,
Confessed and unconfessed,
Through all the corrupted world's disease of soul,
Stands steadfast, staunch

                this joy of one Redeemer.

Therefore, Spirit of Health, Spirit of Healing,
              into thy hands....

Gentle be my going forth
In confident cessation.

Walk Into Daylight

Waking before the sunrise, she and I
Walk the woodland trails, beginning when darkness
Flows flood-tide and sends its somber currents
Billowing over the scarred and sullied earth.
No birds sing in that darkness; only cicadas
Bicker in dissonant shrilling while the night
Dissolves all shapes and forms into obscurity.
We bring a sliver of light, saved from the past,
Something to help us, groping, to find the Path
Winding among dark thickets. Journeying on,
Stumbling at times, sometimes losing the Way,
We walk to the promise of the coming day.

Then comes the gift of the dawn, slowly at first,
Gently diluting the darkness, gaining in strength,
Quietly leavening shadows into lucidity,
Bush and tree with green leaves trembling alive.
Bright birds sing to their mates, and far in the east
A red ball climbs into heaven from whence it came,
Turning to gold as it rises, lighting the Way,
Leading us into our walk with certainty given,
Blaze of enlightenment, all shapes starkly revealed,
Nature flaming in color, pulsing alive,
Resonant now with this harmony, steeped in this Joy.

Someday the night will fall, bringing the shadows
First, then deepening into dark—obsidian world
Where turbid insentience smothers, enveloping all.
Or so some fear. Not we. For then we'll drowse

In ebon opacity none can understand,
Ripening slowly till, certain at last, transformed,
We wake to the Promise. There in that golden time
We'll walk together with many millions more
Into the daylight of eternity.

LaVergne, TN USA
05 May 2010
181629LV00004B/115/P